SOUL NOTES

VOLUME ONE

ADAM MALIK SIDDIQ

Copyright © 2021 by Adam Malik Siddiq.

All rights reserved.

No part of this book may be reproduced in any form or by any electronic or mechanical means, including information storage and retrieval systems, without written permission from the author, except for the use of brief quotations in a book review.

*To my grandfather,
my Baba Jan,
Khaled Siddiq Khan "Charkhi".*

Thank you for all the wisdom, love, laughter, and memories that you shared with me.

CONTENTS

Resilience	1
Choose Wisely	3
Know Thyself	4
The Creator Lives Within Their Creations	6
Transformational Witnessing	8
Free Questioning	9
We're All In Relationship With One Another	10
Matters Of The Mind Are All Illusions	11
We Are The Energies Of Creation	12
Avoiding Darkness Perpetuates Darkness	13
Matter Is Not The Primary Reality	15
(Cour)age	17
Humility	18
Mainstream Media Is Junk Food For The Mind	19
Creativity	20
A World Of Intuition	21
Intimacy: A Dance Between Presence And Openness	22
Normal Sucks	23
You're Not A Failure	25
Practicing Emotions	27
Time Is A Construct	28
Problems Are Messengers	30
Awareness Heals	31
Become Aware Of What Is	32
Gratitude…Just Because	33
When They Say You're "Too Much"	34
Scared Or Sacred?	36
Love Is Indescribable	37
Question	38
Destiny	39
Life's Plans	41
Audit Your Mind	42
Presence Versus Attention	44
Legacy Of Love	45
Abundance Into Scarcity	46
Choose Humility Or Humility Will Choose You	47

The Myth Of Toxic Masculinity And Femininity	48
Say "NO" Effectively	50
Your Time Is Sacred	51
Quality Requires Quality	53
The Gift Of Creation	54
Nature Is Our Medicine	55
From "Depression" to "I Pressed On"	56
Seek Deeper	57
We Are Rivers Streaming Towards The Ocean	58
Greatness Is A Journey, Not A Finish Line	59
Have A Vision So Big That You Lose Yourself In It	61
Unlearning	62
Cutting Cords	63
People Aren't Toxic	65
Asleep Or Awake	67
The Gift From The People We Can't Stand	69
The Best Way To Solve Problems	70
Divide And Rule Or Unite And Love	72
Whatever You Bless Blesses You	73
Romance Isn't Dead	74
Put Your Gifts And Talents To Work	75
Life Is Too Short To Procrastinate Your Purpose	76
Control	77
Bullseye	78
All Of Life Is Interwoven	79
On Living Fully And Wisely	80
Life Doesn't Care About Your Expectations	81
The World Hasn't Gone Mad	83
The wise, the foolish, the lovers, and the mystics	84
Empty Yourself	85
Move Towards	86
Planting The Seeds Of Your Legacy	87
Forget The Cups, Be The Ocean	88
Love Is Your Greatest Adventure	89
Love Is Beyond Understanding	90
Beyond The Matrix	91
Amidst Times Of Great Uncertainty	92
Giving Up Doesn't Mean Losing	94
Problems Are Opportunities	96
The Ambitious One And The Troubled One	97

The Interpreter, The Interpreting, And The Interpretations	99
Simple Acts	101
Our Pains Are Messengers	102
Growth And Adventure	105
The Background	106
Thriving: The New "normal"	107
Confidence Versus Conviction	108
Imagine	109
Vision	110
The Soul's Light	111
Unlearning And Remembering	112
Imagination	113
Finding Your Purpose	114
Consistency	115
When Things Are Falling Apart	116
There's No Lack Of Energy	117
Stuckness	118
Nothing Compares	119
You Have The Power Of Choice	120
Let The Dead Leaves Drop	121
Let Love Rip "You" Apart	122
Union	123
The Eternal Wisdom Within	124
Fear	126
Awareness And Systems	128
Bless Your Problems	131
Why Are You So Concerned With "Being Enough"?	132
Your Purpose Is Who And How You Are	133
Complex Problems Are Comprised Of Simple Patterns	135
Is The Glass Half-Empty Or Half-Full?	136
Find Eternity Within This Moment	137
Mind Must Be Guided By Heart	138
Fitting In	139
Invest Your Time Purposefully	140
Love Guides Us The Right Way	142
Life Interferes With Our Plans	143
Why There's So Much Suffering In The World	144
Greater Consciousness	146
Everyone Is Guided	148
Planting Seeds Of A New Vision	149

Graceful Or Painful Guidance	151
Coherence	152
Your List	153
Parallel Realities	154
Intuition	156
Spiritual Bypass	158
You Don't Need To Prove What You Intuitively Know	160
Humility	161
What Would Love Do?	162
Finding The Extraordinary Within The Ordinary	163
Love Bewilders	164
Harmony	165
Awakening	166
Polish Your Inner World	167
The Trap Of Proving Yourself	169
How To Be A True Rockstar	170
True Success	172
The Game Of The Mind	173
Liberating Stuckness	175
The Illusion Of "Toxic" Masculinity And Femininity	177
Ancestors	179
Amidst Times Of Uncertainty	180
Stretching	182
Happiness	183
Breathing Deep	185
Spirituality	186
This Silence	188
Question What You See And Hear	189
On Proving Others Wrong	191
Time Is Limited	193
Listen To Your Inner Guidance Counselor Frequently	195
The Intent Of The Communicator	196
There Are No Failures, Only Results	197
The Gift Of Your Most Painful Experiences	198
Living Truth	199
Overthinking	200
Embrace Your Pains	202
Travel	204

Synchronicity	206
Observe And Create Rather Than React And Destroy	207
Acknowledgments	209
About the Author	211
Also by Adam Malik Siddiq	213

RESILIENCE

Your resilience, perseverance, and even your ability to thrive in the face of adversity is far greater when you have a vision to live for.

My grandpa was cruelly imprisoned for two decades when he was only six-years-old by a radically corrupt and tyrannical family that stole the throne from the rightful King of Afghanistan (King Amanullah Khan) and sought to exterminate all the intellectuals and influential peoples of Afghanistan, as well as their families, who they saw as a threat in the way of their corrupt regime.

Nadir Shah and his brothers carried out this extermination plan of theirs by way of mass executions and imprisonments.

He faced horrible challenges, saw death many times, and still, he came out of those two decades learning to read, write, and speak six languages fluently, memorizing thousands of poems by the great spiritual masters: including Maulana Jalaluddin Balkhi (Rumi), Hafiz Shirazi, Saadi Shirazi, Shams-i-Tabrizi, Bedil, Jami, and many more.

He also studied all the great eastern and western philosophers.

Having no access to education from the outside world ever, he made it a point to study all day everyday from the wise people who were political prisoners as well.

My grandpa was consistently focused on wanting to do all he could to become a profound and meaningful contribution to his family and countrymen whenever he'd be free from the unjust crimes against humanity imposed upon him and his family.

He had a vision, and this vision empowered him to persistently show up, day after day, with a passion to learn and grow his mind.

CHOOSE WISELY

We're making choices in every moment.
We're choosing what we're focusing on.
We're choosing the quality and quantity of energy we're showing up with.
We're choosing the meaning we give to our experiences.
We're choosing what we tolerate by what we give attention to and the standards we hold ourselves to.

Choosing wisely requires us to act with intentionality, knowing that our choice is not just our personal choice, but also our choice for what we want to see more of in the world.

When we make choices that contribute to the greater well-being of life, we feel most alive and fulfilled.

Choose wisely, my friends.
Humanity depends on it now more than ever.

KNOW THYSELF

When you know yourself so deeply,
the opinions of others will become irrelevant to you.

When we are seeking the approval of another,
it's generally because we are not approving ourself, a symptom of not knowing oneself.

When you truly know yourself,
you will know your Source,
and when you know your Source,
you could care less about the opinions or "judgments" of others.

You care, above all else, about keeping integrity with yourself and your Source.

There's no separateness between one and their Source; they are in unison together.

Here's an example to personify the union:

When someone is playing a video game, they are playing as the character that experiences this virtual world as real...as the only reality in existence. They, however, are the one playing this character, this avatar, experiencing the avatar's world through the focal point of the character.

When we focus inwards to know ourselves, towards the center of our hearts, we transcend the human experience and our virtual reality experience of the world, ascending to the eternal state of consciousness that we truly are. We are all this infinite, eternal consciousness observing itself as we play through this game of life. We are not separate characters, rather unique characters and expressions of the One Consciousness that creates and witnesses all existence.

Know thyself.
Be thyself.
Deeply.
Profoundly.
Vividly.
Vivaciously.
Passionately.
Tenaciously.

THE CREATOR LIVES WITHIN THEIR CREATIONS

Embodied within all creations is their Creator.

Within all the great artworks of Picasso lies the spirit of Picasso.

Within the great architecture of Gaudi is the essence of Gaudi.

Within the Masnavi, we feel the heart of Rumi.

Within the cooking of a loving mother, we taste her motherly love.

Within any creation or work, the essence of the creator or collaborative creators can be felt in its making.

Just as we can experience the essence of the artist, chef, philosopher, poet, or visionary in their creations, think of the divinity that created you…that exists within you as a result.

Maulana Jalaluddin Balkhi (Rumi) and Shams-i-Tabrizi spoke of God existing within our hearts, and that through spiritual companionship, we can experience the opening of this heart-portal.

At the core (heart) of your existence is where God is.

TRANSFORMATIONAL WITNESSING

Most people default to defining reality based on how things are and how they feel; in other words, their circumstances and their reactions to them. Most people forget that we are defining reality moment to moment. When you realize that you're the one choosing your experience in relation to reality, you have awakened the powers of transformational witnessing.

Mystics are masters of witnessing reality. Through witnessing, they are like alchemists, transmuting lead into gold. They can transmute anything into gold because they choose to witness the gold that exists within.

Witness the gold within yourself and others. That's how we create an enriching humanity.

Witness the sacred.

FREE QUESTIONING

If people are unwilling to question what they've been told, are they even free?

Do you own your beliefs or do your beliefs own you?

How willing are you to question what you know?

How willing are you to objectively observe information that contradicts your perspective?

Do you prefer to never question your ideas or are you open and curious to explore what else could be true?

Do you believe everything you're told first or do you question what's really being said behind the words?

Is ignorance bliss or is awareness bliss?

WE'RE ALL IN RELATIONSHIP WITH ONE ANOTHER

All of life is in relationship with all of life, always. We are not separate. We are all interconnected. We are all One through the Light that energizes, creates, and shines through us.

At the core of all pain is experiencing the illusion of separation. Until we accept that we are all One, life will break down the illusory walls of the mind so that we remember our sacred place in the weaving of Creation.

We are all One.
Always.
Nothing in life is separate.

Remembering our oneness is vital for us to realign our ways of life to be in harmony with naturally thriving.

MATTERS OF THE MIND ARE ALL ILLUSIONS

The heart and soul know the truth.

Matters of the mind are all illusions.

Your heart and soul intuit wisdom and truth moment to moment.

Trust that intuitive voice with your life.

It will always guide you towards more love, purpose, joy, growth, contribution, and experiences the mind cannot understand.

WE ARE THE ENERGIES OF CREATION

We are made of the same energies that created the universe.

We are consciousness experiencing being human.

Mastering ourselves is our greatest quest, for it is what leads us to develop mastery of our relationship with the energies of Creation.

Commit to self-mastery.

Let your soul show you the way.

AVOIDING DARKNESS PERPETUATES DARKNESS

Avoiding, ignoring, and suppressing the ugly and dark things happening in the world only allows it to keep perpetuating.

"I just want to focus on positivity."

"I don't want to know about it because I feel like I can't do anything about it."

"It's a waste of time to look into it because there's nothing we can do about it."

Have you heard this from people?

Have you said it yourself?

Avoiding anything somehow always brings us more of what we avoid. Anything we push away with polarity comes back with more force. When we as a humanity turn our cheek to the darkness of the world, it only continues to fester. Evil does not diminish by being ignored; it diminishes by having light shined upon it.

There are many ugly, dark, horrible things happening in the world right now that are affecting millions of people. This includes everything from human trafficking (child trafficking, sex trafficking, organ harvesting, slave trade, etc.), genocide, famine, detainment of innocents, forced labor camps, and more.

Becoming aware of what's happening without any political, religious, or cultural bias is an important first step for all. I say without bias because it's often when observe through our biased lens that we divide ourselves into polarized arguments, rather than uniting together to create new solutions that pull these horrors out from the roots and eradicate the evil sources, ensuring they never happen again.

We can't turn our faces to the darkness. We are meant to be beacons of light. We must shine the light of awareness and truth into where there's darkness. We must bring our gifts abundantly into where there's lack. We must care for others who we'd never meet…for people who could never pay us back. This is the most fulfilling part of what it means to be human: to be a soul.

MATTER IS NOT THE PRIMARY REALITY

Matter is not the primary reality. Energy and consciousness, light and sound, vibration and frequency are what organize no-thing into some-thing. The universe is a living, unified, vibrational reality. Always be intentional of the energies you focus and bring to reality, as well as the consciousness that envelopes your thoughts, ideas, decisions, and emotions. You are creating and being created by energy and consciousness every single moment and you get to choose the quality with your focus.

Cymatics is the study of how sound shapes and organizes matter. Dr. Masaru Emoto studied how particular sounds, names of people, and even thoughts and emotions affected the structure of water by observing the water under a microscope after it was influenced by a certain sound, emotion, or name. When he played Mozart, water organized as a beautiful crystalline structure. When he played death metal, it was disharmonious and vile looking. When he focused on gratitude, it formed a beautiful snowflake-like structure. When he focused on anger, it became another distorted mess.

What we choose to think about and how we choose to feel affects not only our internal reality, but also the external reality and all those who we come in contact with through the energy we transmit. Roughly 60% of our body is made of water, and roughly 71% of the planet is made of water. Live wisely by choosing higher quality thoughts, emotions, and energies, and we can manifest a more enriching quality of life for ourselves, others, and the world.

(COUR)AGE

The root word of courage is "cour", meaning heart.

To act with courage is to act with heart.

An earlier definition of courage meant: to speak one's mind by telling all one's heart.

Bronnie Ware, a palliative nurse, documented in her book, "The Top 5 Regrets of the Dying", that the #1 regret she heard the most was this:

I wish I had the courage to live a life true to myself, not the life others expected of me.

We need so many more courageous people to get humanity realigned with our core/cour/heart right now.

Let's bring about the age of cour…the age of heart…where the heart is what leads us all with the magisterial, harmonic, synergistic rhythms of love.

HUMILITY

Awakening shows us how little we really know, reminding us to always be humble, to question, and to be aware of the divine guidance available in every moment.

Humility creates space for Grace.

MAINSTREAM MEDIA IS JUNK FOOD FOR THE MIND

Consuming information from the mainstream media and thinking you're becoming informed is like consuming fast-food and thinking you're becoming healthy.

Question the source of what you consume and always seek the purest source.

CREATIVITY

That which is organic is innately creative and unique.

Beauty blooms from the free expression of your true self.

Allow the innate creativity to flow through you freely like a river of joy.

A WORLD OF INTUITION

Imagine a world where everybody trusted their intuition.

We can create it.

It starts with ourselves.

Everything we want to see change in the world begins with ourselves.

INTIMACY: A DANCE BETWEEN PRESENCE AND OPENNESS

Intimacy is found in the dynamic between presence and openness.

The deeper the presence, the deeper the openness, the deeper the intimacy, the deeper the fulfillment.

The sun shines its presence at the earth and the earth twists and turns in a glorious unfolding with her lush green dress of trees, flowers, plants, and creatures dancing with life.

The masculine penetrates the feminine with his presence and she welcomes him into the depth which he craves.

The two dance together with romantic synergy,
two becoming One.

NORMAL SUCKS

How is it that we've accepted that it's normal to be stressed out, burnt out, unfulfilled, unhealthy, in major debt, out of harmony with nature, and addicted to our "smart" devices that provably make us dumber the longer we rely on them?

Things aren't going to get any better if we continue allowing ourselves to live with such radical disharmony and neglect.

We need to decide for ourselves first what our standards must be.

Through how we live, we can inspire greater possibilities for others, but we truly only have control over what we commit to do for ourselves.

We can always choose something greater right now.

Every choice made for something greater is a choice made for more than just ourselves individually, because as we become better, our beneficial impact on others and the environment is going to get better.

Every choice we make is something we promote more of for humanity.

YOU'RE NOT A FAILURE

Don't call yourself a failure because you tried to bite off more than you can chew.

Dream and aim big, but know that all great things take time and diligent focus to grow.

Look at yourself.

Think of all the time and energy it took to create you from nothing into human form!

If you have a grand vision, you'll need profound patience coupled with daily progress.

This is a marathon, not a sprint, and it's important to enjoy the views as you're heading towards your destination.

The purpose of your goals is to guide you into new directions, making you greater and more wholesome as you learn more about yourself, all while inspiring new connections along the way.

Don't get so lost that you think the goal is just the goal.

There's always more than just going from point A to point B.

Someone asked me what advice I'd tell them if they wanted to succeed as an entrepreneur but were afraid of failure.

I told them that failure is part of growing.

Just because you've failed to meet your goal within a designated time period does not make you a failure.

Who's to say the true goal was even the goal, whether you were aware of it or not?

Have more faith in how life is guiding you, for life is not going to lead you astray from your purpose.

PRACTICING EMOTIONS

Our experience of reality is colored by the emotions we repetitively practice.

If we're fearful, everything can seem dark.

If we're hopeful, everything can seem possible.

If we're empowered, anything feels possible.

If we're courageous, we're moving forward no matter what.

If we're joyful, magic is in the air everywhere.

If we're grateful, we find gifts everywhere.

If we're passionate, life is music.

What do you choose to practice now?

What emotions must humanity practice more?

TIME IS A CONSTRUCT

Time is a construct. We live in timelessness. Space is an experience. We're created from spaciousness. Things appear solid when they're actually being created and re-created in every moment. Most of your cells are not the same ones from years ago. If you appear to be the same, it's a result of the same energy and consciousness you've chosen over and over and over again.

You say, "How? It's not happening right now!"

It's happening in every moment. How long can you continuously choose the energy and consciousness of that vision? That's what guides everything else to fall into a new place. Enjoy the time it takes to "get there". The time will be filled with all the necessary happenings to "get there".

You're already there when you're envisioning. You're bringing it from no-where to now-here. If you don't know of a greater vision to choose, allow yourself to be chosen by something greater. One way or another, we're always being guided. Whether we listen and act based on life's guidance is another story. When we pay more attention to this sacred mystery, we can move with it, like dolphins riding the waves, like eagles soaring with the grace of the wind.

Choose and be chosen by something greater for life.

PROBLEMS ARE MESSENGERS

We often think the problem at hand is the problem, when it's just a symptom of something deeper and, ultimately, a signal and catalyst for growth, change, and an expansion in awareness.

Problems are messengers.

Pay attention.

Let them teach you.

AWARENESS HEALS

People often don't want to know about the horrors in the world because they feel helpless to do anything about it.

The simple act of becoming aware of what's going on is already an act to change it.

Nothing changes worldwide until enough people become aware of the way things have been.

Nothing heals until we are aware of what needs healing.

And when the light of awareness is shined upon what needs healing, the miracle of life gets to work and mend what needs care.

Our awareness becomes a funnel of energy for that which we focus on.

BECOME AWARE OF WHAT IS

Becoming aware of exactly what's happening is one of the most productive things we could ever do.

Awareness itself is an act of transformation.

Awareness is true bliss, for awareness provides us with the gift of making a difference.

Through bringing more conscious energy and awareness to a problem, we suddenly start to see new solutions emerge and what once felt like friction is beginning to be met with grace as the truth is revealed.

GRATITUDE...JUST BECAUSE

You don't need "stuff" to be grateful for.

You can be grateful without any reason to justify gratitude.

Gratitude is the pulse that beats in our hearts.

Gratitude is the melody of the universe.

Gratitude is our natural state of being.

Gratitude is the joy of witnessing creation.

The idea that we need things to be grateful is the illusion.

Gratitude is a frequency.

WHEN THEY SAY YOU'RE "TOO MUCH"

If being passionately and authentically expressed is "too much" for some people, don't ever get discouraged to dim your brilliance. Brighten it up!

Some people have been living in the shadows for a long time. The light may feel scorching to their lightless eyes at first. Some will complain by reacting or withdrawing, but others will see and thank you as a godsend.

In a society where passion is withheld except for brief moments of celebration, whether it's victories with your favorite sports team, a holiday, or some special moment, we need more wild drunken lovers to awaken the dead fish to the Ocean's drunkenness (the field of Love).

How often do you feel intoxicated by the magical and spontaneous unfolding of life?
How often do you let your heart pour the wine of God (love) through your words freely?
Do you feel free in your body, mind and soul?

Do you feel free in your expression?
If not, who's holding you back?
Who?

SCARED OR SACRED?

The difference between "scared" and "sacred" is how you see the letters organize. How we witness reality influences both how we see and experience it as well as how it organizes. We can turn a disheveled mess into a sacred work of art. All it takes is a greater intention to start.

We can find things that make us feel scared about the world right now, and we can find things that remind us how sacred life is right now. We can choose to bring the sacred into the scared, bringing light to the darkness. First, we must choose the lens we view reality with, and we are all due for a polish. How can we see clearly if the lens isn't polished? We can see a blemish through the glass and mistake it for a monster on the other side.

LOVE IS INDESCRIBABLE

Love is indescribable.

Love is beyond mind.

Love is beyond words, ideas, and senses.

Love is the essence of the essence of all life.

Love is the glue
between me and you.

Love is the inter-weaving and inter-directing
current between us.

QUESTION

The world is not as it appears to be.

Keep your eyes open and question often.

Be aware.

Question.

Question your questions.

DESTINY

Our destiny is shaped in the spaciousness between the meaning we give to life experiences.

Some say, "It's over."
Others say, "It's just begun."
Some say, "My plans were ruined."
Others say, "I've been called for something more."
Some say, "This is the worst thing that's ever happened to me."
Others say, "I'm going to make this the most important thing that ever happened for me and let it serve as a reminder so I can live fully and be more for life."

We always have the gift to choose what things mean. The meanings we choose can energize or drain not only us, but others too. When we choose empowering meanings, when we choose to make unfortunate circumstances a reason for why we will show up more for life, we inspire others.

Oftentimes, the most inspiring people to us are the ones who've gone through Hell and still find joy wherever they are, because eternal joy is within us. In an abundantly energized world, hopefully nobody will ever have to go through Hell to realize that Heaven is here on Earth, within our hearts. In that spaciousness between our choice of meaning, our destiny and our impact to others is shaped. In that spaciousness, allow yourself to choose or be chosen by something greater.

LIFE'S PLANS

We have our plans, and then life has plans for us.

The more we surrender to life's plans, the more effortless, magical, and enjoyable our life becomes.

Be open.

We're guided.

By life, for life.

AUDIT YOUR MIND

How often do you audit your perspectives, beliefs, ideas, concepts, and opinions?

Behind every perspective, belief, value, story, and idea is energy.

The belief becomes a placeholder for a particular quality and quantity of energy, and that energy influences our body, emotions and mind.

When you audit your beliefs, you give yourself the opportunity to go in the space between thoughts and beliefs.

In this spaciousness, you can be with the thoughts without the attachment to them, able to discern the impact of them upon yourself and even others.

When we choose a richer quality of energy, the contents of our life upgrade.

Energy is the source of everything, including the beliefs, ideas, and concepts we choose.

PRESENCE VERSUS ATTENTION

Most people compete for your attention.

Presence is what wins long-term.

Presence is fully witnessing another with depth.

Presence seeks and engages the soul where attention alerts the mind and emotions.

With presence, we transcend the dimension of mind, experiencing eternity in the now.

LEGACY OF LOVE

If we're not in sync with our purpose and our heart, we'll never be fulfilled…regardless of whatever feats we accomplish.

Status, fame, money, cars, homes…none of that stuff comes to the grave with you.

Written on tombstones, the statements read messages like "loving father", "loving mother", "loving grandfather", or "loving grandmother".

True legacy is about love and contribution.

Expand your legacy of love.

ABUNDANCE INTO SCARCITY

Focus on where there's abundance.

Don't dwell on where there's scarcity.

Pour the energy of abundance into where there's scarcity.

Bring the light into the darkness.

You need water to grow plants.

Nobody can grow anything without a source of energy.

This is how we bring blessings…by pouring energy from abundance into scarcity.

Your focus, your observer, is your tool for transforming reality.

Use it wisely.

CHOOSE HUMILITY OR HUMILITY WILL CHOOSE YOU

It's wiser to choose humility than to be humbled by life.

Either way, we're destined to be more for the world.

Some say life doesn't happen to you…that instead, life happens for you.

When you are humble, life happens through you…for you, and for more life.

Choose humility or humility will choose you.

It's an easy choice for the soul, yet a difficult, nearly impossible one for the ego.

THE MYTH OF TOXIC MASCULINITY AND FEMININITY

Masculine energy is not toxic. Feminine energy is not toxic. Masculine and feminine are both aspects of creation. Both need one another. Both complement one another. What is toxic is separating masculine and feminine, vilifying one or the other, creating rules and stories about how they must be, rather than allowing the innate wisdom to be free.

There's no such thing as toxic masculinity and femininity, as masculine and feminine are the energies of creation, irrespective of gender, although they are embodied by gender when we are coherent with our true nature.

The inception of these false ideas were created to demonize the natural essence of life.

Slowly but surely, "they" indoctrinated new generations of men to lose touch with their masculine nature and women to lose touch with their feminine nature.

When you have people losing connection with their natural

essence, you start to get more men behaving like women and women behaving like men.

Both become more stressed, unfulfilled, and unhealthy over time as they continue living incongruent to their true nature.

Hormonal changes begin to take more effect and tragically, today the testosterone and sperm count of men are significantly lower than ever before, unnaturally so, along with more women having fertility issues than ever before.

One has to ask: why?

Everything begins with energy.

When distorted from one's natural essence, the body and mind do not function optimally.

This "toxic" masculine or feminine agenda servers one core reason above them all: to delete our connection with our true nature in order to normalize us to accept a robotic humanity, disconnected from soul, genderless in expression, with our consciousness controlled by Artificial Intelligence, and all that was once natural replaced with a controllable, artificial construct for a "new humanity".

What is evil?

The inversion of live…the inversion of life.

SAY "NO" EFFECTIVELY

NO: a powerful word that, when used effectively, can clear out all distractions from your YES and your destiny.

How often and effectively are you saying "NO"?

YOUR TIME IS SACRED

Value your time as sacred.

Every second that passes is gone forever.

The only thing that lives on is what you create with this time.

There are 86,400 seconds in 24 hours.

When we subtract 6-8 hours of sleep, we're left with 57,600-64,800 seconds to use while we're awake.

How effectively and efficiently we use the time while we're awake directly affects the quality of our lives.

Productivity isn't to be mistaken with always working.

Productivity is measured by our results.

Being busy is often very unproductive and unfulfilling.

Are you creating and enjoying fulfilling experiences in all of your relationships, for your health and life?

We shouldn't be stressed about time.

We should be appreciative of time, and we should maximize it to accomplish and enjoy what matters most to us.

Rather than seeing your time as an expense, see it as an investment.

What is the future legacy you want to invest this second into?

QUALITY REQUIRES QUALITY

Whether it's being a professional athlete, having a phenomenal relationship, or creating an amazingly successful business…quality requires quality.

You get what you put in.

Whether it's your body, mind, family friendships, intimate relationships, business, finances, mission, goals, dreams, or anything else…they all require you invest higher quality energy to grow.

THE GIFT OF CREATION

Nobody, no circumstance, can ever take away your ability to create.

The act of creating is an experience where we become one as the creator, the process of creating, and the creation.

Being aware of this…what do you think you truly are then?

Within the creation is the signature of its Creator.

Within your heart is Love's essence.

NATURE IS OUR MEDICINE

Only in a society so devoid of nature can there be so much discord, disease, disillusionment, destruction, disharmony, and disaster.

We must return to our nature.

We must live from our nature.

We must live in harmony with nature.

It's so simple.

It's so natural.

It's so effortless.

It's so magical.

Nature is our medicine, teacher, guide, and purpose.

FROM "DEPRESSION" TO "I PRESSED ON"

"Depression" becomes "I pressed on" when the letters reorganize.

We transform our experience of reality by how we focus on things.

What you choose to focus on and the meaning that you give to that directly affects your experience and quality of life, which affects others because we're all connected.

SEEK DEEPER

If we questioned why we wanted what we want, would we still want what we want?

How often is desire just driven by an unconscious impulse to fulfill a surface-level need?

Seek deeper.

Question why.

What is it that you're truly seeking?

Why?

Do you want to accomplish this goal because you want to prove others wrong?

Why?

Question the desire behind your desires.

WE ARE RIVERS STREAMING TOWARDS THE OCEAN

We are all rivers streaming to the Ocean.

We are all paths along the Great Journey.

We are all candles lit by the fire of Love.

We are Love embodied within Love's desire.

GREATNESS IS A JOURNEY, NOT A FINISH LINE

There's no finish line for greatness.

There's no final lesson for mastery.

There's no such thing as giving it your all.

There's always more.

We're always capable of being more.

The only limits to your potential are the ones you've allowed yourself to believe.

Every time you choose to be more, you choose more for humanity.

While people didn't believe anyone could run a 4-minute mile, Roger Bannister did.

He saw himself accomplishing it in his mind over and over again.

The year after he did it, a number of others followed the same trail of accomplishment.

Today, high school athletes accomplish that.

The same goes for anything in life.

Life is a journey and how we live it is both our prayer and answer.

HAVE A VISION SO BIG THAT YOU LOSE YOURSELF IN IT

Most of us have been conditioned to believe that productivity is about accomplishing all our tasks, crossing out our to-do lists, and that by being constantly busy, we are being productive.

Productivity is not about how busy we are; it's about the quality results we produce.

When we are clear on our vision and purpose, we will know which outcomes become the necessary targets for our focus.

From there, we know the best decisions to make, tasks to accomplish, and actions to take in order to more efficiently reach our outcomes.

It all begins with having a vision.

Have a vision so big, you lose yourself in it and thus, become it.

UNLEARNING

The only limits to your potential are the ones you've allowed yourself to believe.

Unlearn your way to realizing your potential.

Unlearn all that is not natural and obstructive to your true, liberated nature.

CUTTING CORDS

There is no such thing as cutting cords with people.

Even if you're no longer in contact with them and you believe they're not a part of your life anymore, you're still connected together and the way you think of them affects both of you, even without physical or verbal contact.

It's not about my life and their life.

This experience we all have the gift to experience and share is life.

We're all a part of life.

It's only the mind that make us appear separate, when in reality, we're all interconnected to one another.

Bless your cords by how you think of them.

Your thoughts echo throughout this field of consciousness.

Choose the thoughts humanity needs to think.

Choose thoughts that are coated with love.

PEOPLE AREN'T TOXIC

People aren't toxic. It's the deficiency in quality energy that they have in their bodies, emotions, mind, and spirit that is toxic.

With an upgrade in the quality of choices made for their bodies, emotional states, mental focus, and spiritual connection, suddenly, they're not toxic anymore.

Even the simplest upgrade in their focus can instantly change the trajectory of their life in mountainous ways.

That pivot in focus can happen from the words you consciously speak, the thoughts you consciously think, and the emotions you consciously feel.

Even something as subtle as an expansion in awareness, just being with what is, is enough.

No matter how poor their energy is, we always have the ability to bless the person with something as simple as just focusing on them with well wishes.

To give an example, a Hawaiian doctor named Ihaleakala Hew Len set up an office within a criminally insane mental hospital to review patients' files.

While reviewing their files, he'd repeat a simple Hawaiian prayer known as Ho`oponopono, which means "to make right".

He'd look at their pictures and constantly repeat the four phrases:

> **"I'm sorry.**
> **I love you.**
> **Please forgive me.**
> **Thank you."**

After a few months, the patients who were shackled were allowed to walk freely, other patients were taken off medications, and even the most hopeless cases were eventually released and integrated back into society.

How we focus our attention, energy, and thoughts on others, let alone anything in life, always has a direct affect upon it.

Sometimes it just takes some more time, but that doesn't mean the impact isn't happening.

ASLEEP OR AWAKE

Those who are asleep want to stay asleep.

They will fight to remain asleep if you try to wake them.

So often for the sleeping souls, it isn't until a big storm hits their life, crumbling their cocoon of insulation and comfort, forcing them into deeper introspection so they can finally begin to seek and question what's real.

They may call this period of their life the "dark night of the soul", but there is no darkness with soul: only brilliance.

The dark night was what they were leaving, this state of sleepwalking throughout life.

Once awakened, they won't want to go back to sleep.

They can no longer accept the illusions they once called "reality".

Your wakefulness is needed now more than ever.

Your wakefulness wakes up others without needing to say or do anything.

Pure presence alone makes a glorious difference.

THE GIFT FROM THE PEOPLE WE CAN'T STAND

Sometimes the greatest gift someone gives you is an example of how not to be.

Let the greedy give you more reason to be generous.

Let the hateful give you more reason to be loving.

Let the selfish give you more reason to be selfless.

Let the sick give you more reason to be healthy.

Let the cowardly give you more reason to be courageous.

Let the liars give you more reason to be truthful.

Let the corrupt give you more reason to be righteous.

Let the evil give you more reason to be good.

Let all give you more reason to be greater.

THE BEST WAY TO SOLVE PROBLEMS

The best way to solve problems is not to fight them, but rather to choose and create greater possibilities of life that make the problems incapable of existing in such a terrific reality.

Rather than fighting disease, create the healthiest body and environment.

Rather than fighting poverty, create systems of abundance with an abundance of opportunities.

Rather than fighting hate, create a world of love.

We feed what we focus on.

Go to the root of the problem and expand to a greater vision with more possibilities of thriving.

All problems are a calling to grow, and humanity has a major calling to grow now…and fast!

We must be the health, abundance, love, gratitude, compassion, empathy, and joy we want to see in the world.

It only takes a moment to make a new choice.

What must humanity choose?

Choose that.

DIVIDE AND RULE OR UNITE AND LOVE

Divide and rule: the simplest strategy for the very few to control the very many.

Unite and love: the simplest strategy for all to thrive harmoniously.

It's really that simple.

Choose to participate with that which unites us with love and respect.

Simple as that.

WHATEVER YOU BLESS BLESSES YOU

Whatever you curse…curses you.

Whatever you bless…blesses you.

Whatever energy you give…you receive.

Why waste your time giving anything less than love?

Do you truly want anything less than love?

People are getting what they're giving and complaining about what they're getting, furthering the cycle of what they give and receive.

Upgrade the energy and the content upgrades effortlessly.

ROMANCE ISN'T DEAD

Romance isn't dead.

Romance never dies.

Romance brings the dead to life and the living to paradise.

Allow yourself to be romanced by the creative energies of Life.

If we are receptive and allowing of it, life will always romance us to participate in sharing our gifts and receiving the gifts of others in this grander play of souls.

This life is a symphony and love is the conductor.

PUT YOUR GIFTS AND TALENTS TO WORK

If you're counting on one person, a group of people, a political party, an anonymous team, some hero or group of heroes to eradicate all the world's problems (and yours) while you feel inclined to sit back and wait for things to unfold, you are doing yourself, others, and humanity a tremendous disservice.

Get up and do something constructive about it.

You've got talents and gifts.

Put them to work.

You were born to make a beneficial difference.

LIFE IS TOO SHORT TO PROCRASTINATE YOUR PURPOSE

If you're not focused on serving and blessing others, you're procrastinating on your purpose.

Life is too short to procrastinate on what matters.

With our lifespan being as precious and short as it is, why waste any time on matters that lack purpose and won't serve your legacy?

Legacy is what lives beyond you.

Be so clear on your vision and your purpose to serve others that you don't have any time for procrastination.

There's no reason to procrastinate when you have a clear vision and are living intentionally, aware of the reality that our time is limited.

In the long-term, anything that doesn't support our legacy is just a waste of time.

CONTROL

Your need for control is controlling you.

Surrender to love.

Surrender to growth.

Surrender to oneness.

Surrender to life.

This life is a symphony and love is the conductor.

We must allow love to be the conductor of our thoughts, decisions, and ultimately, our beingness.

BULLSEYE

Narrow your focus
so profoundly
that all you see
is the center of the bullseye.

Be that precise
with your heart's deepest desires.

ALL OF LIFE IS INTERWOVEN

All of our journeys are interwoven.

None are separate.

None are alone.

All are made One through the guiding currents of love.

Empty yourself of yourself so that love can fill the emptiness.

Emptiness is not loneliness.

Emptiness is spaciousness for greater possibilities to fill the space.

ON LIVING FULLY AND WISELY

Death is certain, but whether you'll live fully and wisely begins with how frequently you attune yourself to your heart's inner-knowing.

The heart and soul know.

Always.

LIFE DOESN'T CARE ABOUT YOUR EXPECTATIONS

Life doesn't care about our expectations.

Life just happens, and the better we are at accepting and adapting, the more graceful and effortless our experience of life becomes.

Either we accept reality for what it is and bless it with more energy, or we argue with reality for not meeting our expectations and neutralize our capacity to make any sort of meaningful impact.

Rather than arguing with the way things are, see them for what they truly are.

Peel back the curtain and see what lies behind the existing conditions.

Acceptance doesn't mean we are tolerant of allowing it to go on longer; acceptance means we accept that this is the way things are, we see the underlying issues that led to this, and rather than fighting with the reality of what's happening, we accept that this is what's happening and we'll choose to bless this situation however we can, allowing ourselves to be purposefully guided to making the greatest difference for ourselves and others.

Whether it's your experience of health, finances, relationship, or your experience of the state of the world, nothing can sustainably change until we uncover why things are the way they are and we come to terms with the reality that this is how the show has been running…until now.

What determines how everything runs is the quality and quantity of coherent energy in the background, as well as the quality of consciousness that we observe with.

Then, with that full picture, we can choose greater possibilities that benefit us all…possibilities that are in sync with life's natural rhythms.

These possibilities always begin with more depth in consciousness and a more quality baseline of energy for how we live our lives.

THE WORLD HASN'T GONE MAD

It's not that the world has gone mad, but that the madness is coming to the surface and being revealed more.

Pull out the weeds so that the garden of love can flourish.

THE WISE, THE FOOLISH, THE LOVERS, AND THE MYSTICS

The wise speak with their presence.

The foolish speak with their tongues.

The lovers speak with their hearts.

The mystics speak with their emptiness.

And then there are some who are wise mystical lovers who foolishly pour out the heart's content: poets.

EMPTY YOURSELF

Empty yourself so that a new you can emerge.

Emptiness creates space for new possibilities to emerge and manifest.

Empty yourself of yourself and let Love transform you into its richly potent and divinely embodied wine.

MOVE TOWARDS

It's easier and more energizing to move towards what you truly desire than it is to move away from what you wish to avoid.

Be clear on what you want.

Question yourself if that's really what you want.

Question how this will benefit others.

Move in the direction where desire and contribution grow together; that's your greatest destiny.

PLANTING THE SEEDS OF YOUR LEGACY

It's never too early to begin planting the seeds of your legacy, and never too late to get started now.

Legacy is not meant to be left for "someday".

Although our time is limited, we live beyond our lifespan through the contributions we make to others.

FORGET THE CUPS, BE THE OCEAN

Why are you so obsessed with this idea that you have to fill your own cup first before you can fill the cups of others when we are swimming in the ocean of Love and our Source is infinite?

Forget the cups.

Be the ocean and be moved by the ocean.

LOVE IS YOUR GREATEST ADVENTURE

Do not mistake comfort for love or you'll miss out on the greatest adventure of your life.

Comfort keeps you where you are.

Love takes you on epic journey.

LOVE IS BEYOND UNDERSTANDING

Love is so profound, it can never be fully described nor understood.

Even the greatest poets can only detail aspects of Love and the intoxicating wondrous trance it allures them into.

Imagine something so great that we can never wrap our heads around it, so profound that it wakes us up and transforms our lives in a moment, and so dear that it lives in the hearts of us all.

BEYOND THE MATRIX

The soul is not confined to the same limits as the body.

It roams between worlds.

It soars throughout dimensions.

It can send its kiss to another who's in another place.

It can bless people while you're even asleep, and long after you're dead.

It can see what the eyes can't see, hear what the ears can't hear, smell what the nose can't smell, feel what the body can't touch, and taste what the tongue can't taste.

It always knows the truth and seeks to liberate others from illusions, freeing them to the magic of life..

We must allow our souls to free our minds of concepts, ideas, thoughts and beliefs, so we can beat with the pulse of Love.

AMIDST TIMES OF GREAT UNCERTAINTY

Amidst these times of great uncertainty, chaos, crisis, and challenge, we must choose to unite and strengthen our bonds with one another even more so.

This is not the time to cut cords; such a thing is an illusion to begin with since we're all connected through this sacred experience we call life.

This is the time to discover new strands and new threads on our already existing cords, as well as discover the cords we haven't noticed before that are pulling our souls forward to new friendships.

This is not the time to, at the drop of a hat, make enemies with our once dear family and friends.

This is the time to both support and grow our relationships with family and friends, as well as expand our circle.

Mostly everybody is enduring the challenges that have come as a result of the combination of circumstances these past two years have presented us with; if not personally, they may be seeing their family or friends experiencing hardships.

While much of the world has been downsizing operations, we must remember not to be downsizing our love, joy, passion, energy, and zest for life.

GIVING UP DOESN'T MEAN LOSING

Some people live their lives swimming against the ocean's currents while reminding themselves to never give up.

No matter how hard and persistently they swim, even with all the effort they exert, they seem to never get closer to what they seek.

If this is you, pray that the Ocean of life sweeps you away and takes you into the direction your soul must venture.

How do you know that where you're being guided isn't better than where you're struggling to swim towards?

Give up to become not just a part of the Ocean, but in your oneness, the entire Ocean too as you're completely in sync and guided.

Giving up doesn't mean losing.

Giving up means opening ourselves up to greater, purposeful, synergistic possibilities that serve us and others much more greatly, effectively, efficiently, and sustainably.

PROBLEMS ARE OPPORTUNITIES

Every problem is an opportunity to grow and contribute more.

Rather than complaining about these problematic opportunities, accept them as quests towards greater destinies.

Right now, in these problematic times, dwells the opportunities for the greatest growth and transformation humanity has yet to experience...just waiting to be discovered and fulfilled.

THE AMBITIOUS ONE AND THE TROUBLED ONE

It matters not if someone who's troubled is surrounded by an abundance of resources and wise people if they're not open to receiving.

It matters not if someone who's ambitious is surrounded by a deficit of resources and wise people if they're open to receiving.

The troubled one continues to find reasons to be troubled and the ambitious one continues to find reasons to be ambitious.

The troubled one is surrounded in fresh springs and complains about there not being enough water while the ambitious one tastes the entire fresh stream in a single drop of water.

You can't help those who aren't receptive to being helped.

Life will give them what they consistently focus on, as well as what they tolerate.

The ambitious ones taste the nectar of life even in a drought where the complainers are blind to realize the miracles all around them.

THE INTERPRETER, THE INTERPRETING, AND THE INTERPRETATIONS

We must become aware of our interpretations of reality and not mistake them as solid, concrete, and unchangeable.

Who's to say the lens you have been viewing reality from is even yours?

Ignore those interpretations of others.

Get to know the interpreter.

The (in)terpreter.

That's who holds the key to all interpretations.

In every moment, there is an interpreter interpreting an interpretation of this experience we call reality.

Most get trapped in the interpretation.

Some are actively interpreting.

Few have, at this point, realized that they are the interpreter interpreting interpretations.

We are the observer observing observations.

Don't get hooked in the observations.

Live from this ever-transformational field of infinite possibilities as the observer, then choose thrones that benefit life.

SIMPLE ACTS

Don't underestimate the impact of how simple acts that build progress steadily towards your goals, visions, and dreams can have on yourself and others.

A mighty tree started once as a seed from the product of another tree, which was once a seed from the product of another tree, and so on.

What we have today is thanks to those who came before us, and what those after us will have will be thanks to what we create and contribute in our lifetimes…starting now.

Simple acts done consistently have the power to build incredible things.

What simple acts can you practice daily that will build upon your goals, dreams, and visions?

What about for your hopes for humanity?

OUR PAINS ARE MESSENGERS

The pains we feel have messages for us.

The metaphors we create affect our experience of life.

You live your life feeling like you're carrying the weight of many on your shoulders, and at the same time, your shoulders feel like they're "killing" you.

You live your life feeling like you're stuck in your head overthinking everything, and at the same time, you've got a headache.

You live your life feeling like you're tight on time, and at the same time, you feel like your upper neck is tense.

You live your life feeling so angry and betrayed, and at the same time, you feel intense pain at your lower neck.

You live your life feeling like you can't move about life authentically, and at the same time, your pelvic and hips feel tight.

You live your life feeling like you can't speak up and voice the truth, and at the same time, your throat feels constricted.

You live your life feeling like you're unsupported, and at the same time, your knee feels weak.

Listen to these pains.

They have wisdom and are here to help us change the course of our lives to become healthier, more vibrant, aware, and wholesome expressions of ourselves.

Acknowledge your pains.

Acknowledge how the way you're living your life, what you focus on and the meanings you've given your experiences have affected your body, emotions, mind and soul.

Bring voice to these pains…these messengers.

That's how all the different signals that we call pain are released and integrated, allowing us the opportunity to make healthy changes efficiently.

Here's a simple exercise you can practice right now if you're in pain:

1. Place your hands on an area where you have the most pain.
2. Breathe into the painful area and let the pain make its sound through your voice as you exhale.
3. Close your eyes and feel if that physical sensation and emotional tone had a color, what would it be?
4. Search around your body, it can be nearby, where you have a painless spot. You might feel peace,

calm, relaxation, joy, or something else that's feels great.
5. Close your eyes, breathe deep, and make the sound of that great feeling as you visualize its color expanding in that spot and all around your body.
6. Now breathe again in the great feeling spot and on your exhales, move your hand and the sound vibration to the area of pain.
7. Do this a few more times, going from the great feeling area to the painful area, and then check on that area where there was pain. What do you feel there now? What color do you feel? What's the quality of the sound that emanates through that part?

Pain is a signal that wants to be heard.

It gets louder the more it gets isolated and ignored.

When it's fully heard, it's integrated.

It doesn't take a lot to fully listen to the signal of pain and receive its wisdom.

It just takes patience and curiosity.

GROWTH AND ADVENTURE

Growth and adventure are essential to a fulfilling life.

Everyday is a new adventure.

Everyday is a new opportunity to grow.

Every outward adventure brings you inward.

Every inward adventure compels you to bring more presence and purpose outwards.

What're you waiting for?

Go venture with joy as your guide.

THE BACKGROUND

How deep is your breathing?

Where is your focus?

What are you thinking about?

What is the meaning you're giving to what you're presently focused on?

How is your posture?

How energized do you feel?

How energized are those around you and those you're in contact with?

How often are you bringing awareness to the subtle factors that affect the quality of your experiences in life?

Bring more attention to what's happening in the background before you allow yourself to get hooked in the foreground.

THRIVING: THE NEW "NORMAL"

We need to make thriving the new normal.

Thriving isn't a complicated science.

We look outside at nature, untouched by mankind, and it thrives beautifully.

Simple shifts aligned with nature and in harmony with our environment and planet sustained over a period of time will create an amazing transformation.

To thrive requires us to be fully connected, harmonious, and energized with our true nature.

CONFIDENCE VERSUS CONVICTION

Confidence is something one builds through experiences over time, but to truly know yourself, that gives you a power that's divine, far beyond the sense of confidence.

Conviction is free of doubt.

Conviction just knows truth.

Take that profound journey deep within yourself and truly get to know thyself.

Know the truth of your nature and no doubts can fog your vision.

IMAGINE

Imagine what could happen
if 3 billion people
all prayed together
in unison,
synced together
at the same time,
for a more healthy,
loving,
abundant,
prosperous,
joyous,
and united
humanity.

VISION

A lack of focus is a symptom of a lack of vision.

When you have an inspiring vision, you are compelled into action.

If you're struggling to focus on task and make progress, it's not about the task, it's about whether you feel connected with your vision and fueled by the purpose this action plays in it.

Give yourself the time to dream as grand as you want and feel the sensations of what creating and bringing that vision into reality will do for others and yourself.

Allow these empowering emotions, fueled by your purpose, to propel you into massive action.

When there's passion, there's focus.

THE SOUL'S LIGHT

Stuck in the patterns of thought,
the soul comes in and pierces the fog
so we can see the truth,
feel the love,
and know ourselves.

The soul's light is unstoppable.
Nothing can hide from it.
It is the light of truth
and it takes no prisoners.
All that is an illusion
is vanquished before its presence.

UNLEARNING AND REMEMBERING

Just because you've practiced living a certain way for so long and become comfortable with it doesn't mean it's your optimal strategy of life.

We must be open to growing and improving, and sometimes that involves unlearning.

We must unlearn what doesn't serve ourselves and others by remembering what naturally serves ourselves and others.

IMAGINATION

Imagination is a portal between non-existence and existence.

To create an abundantly thriving humanity in harmony with nature, we must first imagine it within ourselves.

There are no chokeholds to imagination other than those you impose upon it.

Imagine big and beautifully.

FINDING YOUR PURPOSE

Forget about this quest to find your purpose.

Bring purpose to this moment and each subsequent moment.

You are the purpose.

Bring more of you into every moment.

That's how you fulfill "your purpose".

CONSISTENCY

Consistency and persistency are two of the most underrated attributes one can possess amidst this instant gratification culture that has swept society into thinking it can and must have whatever it wants right now.

Brick by brick, great castles are made.

Step by step, great journeys are made.

Word by word, great books are made.

Building anything great begins with a decision and follows with the simple actions taken moment by moment, minute by minute, hour by hour, day by day, and so on.

WHEN THINGS ARE FALLING APART

What if what's falling apart is falling apart so that something greater can fall into place magically, synchronistically, and effortlessly?

Welcome the greater and it will naturally replace the lesser.

THERE'S NO LACK OF ENERGY

There's no lack of inspiration.

There's no lack of creativity.

There's no lack of energy.

It's just you getting in the way of the natural flow of life.

How can we unstuck ourselves?

Take a breath, acknowledge where you feel stuck, and let go.

You can't force life.

You can't force a miracle.

You simply allow it to happen and witness the happening.

We exist amidst this cosmic electromagnetic field.

How could there ever be lack when our source is infinite?

STUCKNESS

Stuckness is self-imposed.

We make ourselves stuck by focusing on one perspective of how things are, unwilling to see things differently or other perspectives simultaneously.

What more can this mean?

Is this even a meaning that I've discovered and chosen by myself, or is it inherited from my culture or society?

If so, is it empowering and enriching?

Ultimately, it's us who chooses the meaning to life.

It's best we choose meanings that empower us and others.

What meanings have you adopted as your own that come from your family, culture, or society, that have been limiting your ability to experience more love, growth, contribution, joy, gratitude, peace, and an overall beautiful quality of life?

NOTHING COMPARES

Nothing compares to feeling
the breeze of the night,
witnessing the stars glimmering bright,
and while the city sleeps,
feeling like you have God all to yourself.

YOU HAVE THE POWER OF CHOICE

Impatient.
I'm patient.

Impossible.
I'm possible.

Impotent.
I'm potent.

You have the power of choice.

Choose wisely.

The meanings we choose
can empower or disempower us.

All transformation begins
with a change in meaning.

LET THE DEAD LEAVES DROP

Let the dead leaves drop
so the tree can be renewed with life.
Out with what doesn't serve life.
In with what brings more life.
Everything has its season,
and each season is to be respected.

Winter is not the end.
Winter lays the ground for new beginnings.
Winter brings us closer with those most close to us.
Winter tests our resilience.
Winter is a time of reflection.
There's no hiding from winter.
Like a storm,
winter will shake the tree of our life
and make all the dead leaves drop.

LET LOVE RIP "YOU" APART

Love rips us apart so we can remember that
we are the creative magic of the divine
embodied for a short time
to light the world with magic
and revel with joy
in this symphonic harmony
of all things and non-things
that we call the Uni-verse.

Let Love rip "you" to shreds until,
like a grain of salt,
you dissolve in this sea of majesty,
remembering your sacred place
in this shared experience we call "life",
and how all of us are part of this One field,
One consciousness,
One love.

UNION

Union
U n I one
You and I One

When Masculine and Feminine remember
and embrace in union together,
we experience the Oneness of creation.

May all our unions be blessed and bless life.

THE ETERNAL WISDOM WITHIN

Why are you anxiously looking outside of yourself
when there is an eternal well of wisdom
dwelling within you?

Be still.
Be quiet.
Feel the source of all intuition within you.
Then, ask.

In your stillness,
The entire universe is listening from within.
Whatever you want is within you already.

You want to go travel and yet,
the greatest adventure of your life
is knowing yourself.

You want the love of another and yet,
the source of all love
is within you.

You want to change your life and yet,
within you is the mirror
through which you witness life.

Change yourself
and you change your experience of life.

Be still
and seek the answers
from the eternal presence
that dwells within.

FEAR

Fear is a primal emotion encoded within us to help us become aware of impending danger so that we can take immediate action for our physical survival.

Fear is not meant to be ignored, nor is it meant to be conquered.

Fear is meant to be respected.

Realize it's designed to save life.

It's important to distinguish the difference between primal fear and the anxieties of the mind.

Anxiety is the obsessive thinking and worrying of "what if this happens", with the majority of "what if" scenarios having nothing to do with a threat to our physical body and life.

Fear is not something to be overcome.

Fear is something to be respected because fear can save your life.

Anxiety, on the other hand, is a waste of time and drains energy.

We feed whatever we pay attention to with energy, and energy is what makes anything persist and grow.

Recognize anxiety for what it is and then throw your worries away by replacing your focus with faith.

The primal instinct we call fear is our friend, not our enemy, and it calls us to immediate action to ensure our survival.

Listen to your fears.

Don't ignore them.

Don't fight them.

They have wisdom to share with you.

Fear is an instinctual, primal, and necessary emotion we have for our survival.

Fear is physical, embodied, and warns us and others of imminent danger.

Fear is real; anxiety is an illusion.

Respect fear; throw out the anxiety.

AWARENESS AND SYSTEMS

When you observe just the parts of life, you become aware of the dimension of reality where there are just separate individual parts.

When you observe the way the parts connect, collaborate, conflict, and work together, you become aware of two dimensions — where the parts are separate individuals, as well as the space between them where the interactions happen.

When you observe the system as a whole, you become aware of multiple dimensions that include the organizing powers that choose the parts and how they function or dysfunction together, what the purpose is, why they function or dysfunction the way they do, and how they affect the nature of the individual parts.

The problems we see in our world are often diagnosed as an issue with the part or parts, and maybe at best, how the parts are functioning.

Rarely are we taught or shown to look at the system as a whole and see at what quality of energy, consciousness, and integrity the system is functioning by.

A simple tweak in the system can cause a radical change in the way the parts collaborate with one another, as well as the integrity of the individual parts as well.

The vision of an organization has the power to inspire and align the entire team to operate with higher performance, create greater innovations, and serve with more energy and enthusiasm.

With a greater vision, fitness and nutrition strategies, mindset, and plan, one can transform their health and body more effectively and efficiently than just going through the motions.

With a greater mission, synergistic focus, and absolute determination, small teams of people can accomplish life-changing feats that benefit millions of people.

Imagine how a society of people focused on a vision that includes all of us thriving would organize the way we interact and collaborate with one another, and how that will transform all of our lives.

To install a thriving platform for humanity, what we need is more people focused on the systems of our society to see the context that's determined the ways they've operated, why they've operated that way, how it's worked wonderfully, how it's failed, and how the best aspects of it can merge with greater possibilities for how the system can more effectively, efficiently, and sustainably serve all the parts optimally, where the previous system's problems become nonexistent or very rare in occurrence.

Focus on the context behind the system.

One small upgrade to the context of the system, often an intangible upgrade, a shift in awareness, can cause all the parts of the system and the ways in which they function to transform radically.

If we want to change the world, we must focus on our systems and begin by upgrading the context, purpose, energy, and consciousness that orchestrates, directs, and guides the functioning of the entire system.

BLESS YOUR PROBLEMS

All problems are calling us to upgrade the quality of how we're perceiving, organizing, and running our lives.

All problems are calls for expanding our awareness so that we can sync in harmony with the evolution that's ready for us now.

Bless your problems, don't curse them.

They're there to help you grow, and when you grow, we grow.

WHY ARE YOU SO CONCERNED WITH "BEING ENOUGH"?

Why are you so concerned with "being enough" when your source is infinite?

Why are you so concerned with the opinions of others when all that matters is if you fulfilled your purpose?

Why are you so concerned with these pestering thoughts when they're not even your own?

Why are you so concerned with anything since all is in Love's Hands?

Your source is infinite.

YOUR PURPOSE IS WHO AND HOW YOU ARE

Your purpose isn't some mission statement or a one-liner you tell people.

It isn't a single task or some business or non-profit you need to create, nor is it some huge feat or accomplishment.

It isn't your career and it isn't necessarily about any particular thing you do.

Your purpose is in "how" you do what you do.

It's found in the space between yourself and others, how you bless them, receive their blessings, and receive them as a blessing.

Purpose is what you bring to the moment, not something you have to go searching for.

Who you are, how you are, and who you become is your purpose.

To all those who feel like you need to find your purpose, save yourself the time and realize you are the purpose.

You just need to show up truly and fully as yourself.

COMPLEX PROBLEMS ARE COMPRISED OF SIMPLE PATTERNS

The problems that we think are most complex are often a simple pattern played out over and over and over again.

Choose a greater quality of energy and you'll see a greater array of choices that you weren't previously aware of spontaneously emerge as your awareness expands.

The moment you focus on a greater choice, the previous pattern becomes obsolete.

You break patterns by making greater choices consistently, installing greater patterns that are guided by a greater energy in replacement of the lesser ones.

IS THE GLASS HALF-EMPTY OR HALF-FULL?

Forget about the glass being half-full or half-empty.

Direct your focus within.

That's where you'll find the eternal spring, from which you can always bring fullness to whatever you focus upon.

Within your heart dwells the Eternal Presence.

FIND ETERNITY WITHIN THIS MOMENT

Some people walk around seeing everything through the lens of the past while others walk around seeing everything from the lens of the future.

Both miss out on experiencing the spectacular magic of this very moment, so unique that it can never be remembered nor envisioned with the fullness of what it contains.

Eternity exists within this moment.

Experience it.

MIND MUST BE GUIDED BY HEART

No matter how set our mind is at something, if it's not in sync and guided by our heart, we will surely experience pain, frustration, and a lack of fulfillment along the way.

When we impose and force our ideas onto what's meant to happen naturally, there's bound to be friction.

There's a natural order to life, an energetic field that connects all living things, and through the heart, we synchronize with this field, thus synchronizing with life.

Make sure that mindset is guided by the heart, or it'll just keep you busy at best...that is, busy until life humbles you by breaking your heart open so that you remember what must be in charge.

FITTING IN

A word of advice to all those who feel like they struggle to fit in: don't.

Why are you so concerned to fit in when you were born to stand out as a shining example for something greater and more wholesome?

Why ever deny the authenticity of your nature to receive conformity's nod of approval?

If you see, think, feel, know, act, and are different, it's not because something's wrong with you, but rather that your uniqueness adds to the completeness of the melting pot of creation.

Embrace and celebrate your uniqueness and the uniqueness of others.

By doing so, we embrace the oneness of all creation.

Don't fit in; be exceptionally YOUnique.

INVEST YOUR TIME PURPOSEFULLY

Our time is our most precious resource.

We don't know how much we have left.

We don't know when our time is up.

Don't waste it on anything or anyone that's not worth the investment.

Don't kill your time.

You'll never get it back.

How you spend each moment will either cultivate a more prosperous future or one filled with regret.

Everyday is a blessing where you get the opportunity to invest your time wisely, joyfully, and purposefully.

Invest your time.

Don't waste it.

Don't kill it.

Don't even spend it.

Invest it into growth, legacy, enjoyment, love, passion, adventure, and fulfillment.

LOVE GUIDES US THE RIGHT WAY

Love will always guide us in the right direction.
Love will always bring us home,
and bring others with us along the way.
Your heart knows the right decision.

LIFE INTERFERES WITH OUR PLANS

Life is always interfering with our plans, but most people call it an inconvenience or a pain in the ass.

We must be more attentive to life's interferences, for they come with great purpose.

What if the interference is an intervention, and what if that intervention saved you from a path less fortunate?

Stop cursing what has interrupted your plans; perhaps it came with great purpose.

WHY THERE'S SO MUCH SUFFERING IN THE WORLD

Someone asked me why there's so much suffering in the world.

I said to them that it's because we have forgotten we're all interconnected.

Separation is at the core of all suffering.

The illusion of separation, that is.

We're all interwoven, and all the parts of us are interwoven.

We must reclaim the integrity within ourselves to inspire integrity amongst the world.

Reclaim integrity for yourself, and as a byproduct, that will inspire a more integral world as you become an example of integrity and wholeness.

We are all One, and within each of us is a collective of aspects, parts, and versions of ourselves.

We are so much more than a personality, a concept, or an emotion.

Our authentic self is not just one version; it's the wholesomeness and integrity with all of ourselves.

Know yourself, be yourself, own yourself.

GREATER CONSCIOUSNESS

If humanity realized that we're all cut from the same fabric of Creation and viscerally felt our oneness, we wouldn't tolerate hundreds of millions of people starving, living without clean water in impoverished situations, or any of the other tragedies and hardships that affect so many people.

Unfortunately, many believe in the illusion of separation, further insulating themselves, when the truth is that we are interdependent amongst each other, nature, the ecosystems, Earth, and the cosmos.

All of our sufferings are a direct result and portrayal of the quality of consciousness that we've tolerated to run our species.

All of our problems are calling us to upgrade our consciousness.

Consciousness is the operating system of life.

To have greater systems, we must have greater consciousness.

EVERYONE IS GUIDED

Everyone is guided purposefully and this guidance unfolds mystically, magically, effortlessly, and gracefully, so long as we listen and act on our intuition — what our soul directs — swiftly.

We can be guided gracefully or painfully depending on how receptive and active we are with our inner-knowing.

It's much wiser to be receptive and move with the current of grace, especially if you seek more of life's wonder and adventure.

PLANTING SEEDS OF A NEW VISION

Every thought, emotion, decision, and meaning we focus on affects not just ourselves, but so many others as well.

We must be the change we want to see in the world by blessing an enriching vision with our focused attention.

Every time we do this, we send forth ripples of blessings.

You can't expect anything to change if you keep focusing on things the same way.

You must rise above by acknowledging things as they are, as well as expanding your awareness and choosing something greater to replace it with.

How could you ever begin a journey if you're unwilling to step forward?

How could you ever grow a tree if you're unwilling to plant a new seed?

Plant the new seeds for a vision that makes the problems irrelevant and the reality enriching.

Water these seeds with your focus daily.

GRACEFUL OR PAINFUL GUIDANCE

We can be guided gracefully or painfully depending on how receptive and active we are in what our soul directs.

Better to go along easily with what your soul directs than to be swept towards your destiny painfully while you try to cling onto your comfort zone.

COHERENCE

All of life is interconnected through this quantum field.

Our primary language is energy.

When we are integrally and coherently attuned, we intuit the invisible electromagnetic waves in the field around us.

Want to increase your intuition?

Increase your connectivity within yourself by being with all of yourself.

When you're integrated, one coherent being, the channel is clear to receive the insights and downloads from the quantum field as your soul is guided more gracefully through your awareness of life's synchronicities and serendipities.

YOUR LIST

If you're always looking for what's on your list, you'll miss out on the magic that's all around you.

Don't get so lost in searching for what you want that you miss out on the awe of the moment…right here and now.

Amidst all the mundanity and seemingly ordinary, when we're curious and look deeper, we'll find the extraordinary.

PARALLEL REALITIES

There are so many parallel realities and the one we choose to focus on is the one we experience as "real".

Every choice brings us to a different destination.

We can always influence both our future and past with the decisions we make in the moment and the meanings we choose to depict our experience.

How?

Meaning is the color palette to life.

When we have a more enriching meaning replace a disempowering meaning for a past event, we are invigorated with more energy and possibility.

Free from our previous disempowering story for our reality, we are no longer burdened and encumbered by a lesser quality baseline of energy for our life.

In turn, this influences our future because we are now liberated with more energy, passion, and power to move towards a greater goal.

When we realize we are the meaning-makers, we are no longer bound by circumstances, as we get to choose what we make of it…first by what we make it mean.

There's so much more to reality than meets the mind.

Every moment presents a new opportunity to choose something greater to manifest into existence from non-existence.

The wisdom you've spent your life seeking has always been within the core of "you".

From within, new realities come out.

INTUITION

Intuition is basically rapid information processing and pattern recognition powered by a wisdom and operating system that's more profound than the mind...the soul.

While the mind seeks to figure things out and come to conclusions through linear thinking, the soul just knows, sees and feels truth without needing any steps in thinking to come to that discovery.

Truth is something obvious for the soul to recognize, because one of the qualities of the soul's essence is pure truth.

When people say they want to live their truth, what's really calling them is to live with the guidance of their soul more consciously.

They realize that they can no longer show up inauthentically, conditioned by the aspects of their cultural and societal programming that suppress their true nature, and that their life must be lived to serve a bigger purpose.

The only way they'll serve that bigger purpose is if they illuminate what's true…for others and themselves.

Regardless of what the circumstances appear to be, always have faith in your soul.

It always knows what's needed, where you're guided, and what's true.

The soul's wisdom is a beacon of light that not even all the darkness can put it out.

SPIRITUAL BYPASS

Spirit bypasses the mind and all its barriers to get to the core of what's real, illuminating us with the magic of life.

There's no hiding from the soul, no games that can be played like the ego.

It's pure revelation.

It brings us to full experiencing.

This term "spiritual bypass" has been used to define the act of avoiding reality by using spiritual concepts that are out of integrity with the true experience.

The irony is there's nothing spiritual about bypassing reality with these mind-made concepts.

Spirit bypasses all walls, barriers, stories, concepts, and limitations, illuminating and liberating truth and the magic of life.

Spirit bypasses all bullshit to wake us up.

I propose the term "conceptual bypass", since that's the reality of what's happening with people who are "spiritual bypassing".

Rather than being with state of reality, they retreat to their rehearsed idealistic thoughts to provide them insulation from the experiences they want to avoid.

Spiritual intelligences operate in dimensions beyond the mind.

Thus, the mind cannot understand them.

The spiritual energies can only be known through experience.

How to experience them, you ask?

Start by becoming aware of how everything in life around you and within you is so magically organized…or better said, electro-magnetically synchronized.

What you bring attention to expands in sync with the amount of attention you bring to it.

Curiosity opens the dimensions to learn through intuition.

YOU DON'T NEED TO PROVE WHAT YOU INTUITIVELY KNOW

You don't need to prove what you intuitively know to yourself.

You don't need to figure out how you intuitively know.

You just need to trust what you intuitively know, and in that faith, what's true will be revealed before you.

Faith lights the way into the unknown.

Spontaneously, information appears to you magnetically that reveals the "how" to the "what" you intuit, as well as "why" you've intuited it.

After all, we live in an electromagnetic reality.

Information is magnetic to the energy that complements it.

HUMILITY

Either we choose humility or we will be humbled over and over again until we choose humility over and over again.

When we're humble, we allow the energies of Creation to guide us.

We're always being guided to be more, give more, love more, contribute more, enjoy more, appreciate more, and grow more.

Humility creates a portal for the power of infinity to work through us.

WHAT WOULD LOVE DO?

Asking ourselves this question will never lead us astray:

What would love do?

When you're lost...

When you're stuck...

When you don't know what to do...

Ask yourself, what would love do?

Then, do that.

Simple, and it works wonderfully.

FINDING THE EXTRAORDINARY WITHIN THE ORDINARY

Amidst all the mundane and seemingly ordinary, when we're curious and look deeper, we'll find the extraordinary.

The extraordinary is found past the illusion of what we call ordinary.

See something or someone newly with more full perspective.

Recognize the uniqueness of this moment.

Feel the air you breathe and what a gift it is.

Lose your mind in the awe of what created all of this.

Lose yourself in the field of consciousness that created you.

LOVE BEWILDERS

Love bewilders the mind and guides the soul.
Love is not meant to be understood.
Love is meant to be experienced.
Love surrounds us like an ocean and floods us from within.
Love is your beginning and your end.
Love is the essence of your soul.
Love is the essence of the universe.
To know yourself is to know Love.

HARMONY

The fragmentation we see within humanity originates from within us, not from outside events and circumstances.

Polish the mirror within you and you'll see the reflections more clearly.

A world of outer harmony begins with a world of inner harmony.

When we're harmonious and integral with ourselves, we can polish the space between ourselves and connect with each other through love.

After all, love is the conductor of life.

We need only to clear our inner-channel so that love can be the guiding energy for all of us.

AWAKENING

Awakening involves both the realization of the matrix and the true nature of reality that's behind this veil.

We have to see what has programmed us as well as the reality that exists beyond the programming.

POLISH YOUR INNER WORLD

If we are troubled, we will perceive the outside world as troubled; as a result, we will continue to find more reasons to feel troubled.

If we are lively, we will perceive the outside world as lively; as a result, we will continue to find more reasons to feel lively.

If the lens through which we see the world is left unchecked, we will continue to see the world based on the emotions, thoughts, and world-views we've rehearsed the most, often the ones we've been conditioned by culture and society to abide by in order to receive acceptance, validation, and likability.

If we polish our inner-selves, the lens through which we see the world is much clearer.

Our ability to discern what is and what isn't becomes sharper.

We interpret the information of the outer world based on our experience within our inner world.

To truly have a world of outer harmony, we must all do our due diligence to polish our inner world.

We polish our inner world by first becoming present and aware of our observations.

When we realize we are not the observations, but the observer observing the observations, we are no longer bound by the energy of what's being observed.

Remembering our power as the observer, we can choose greater states of being to experience, irrespective of the circumstances the outer world presents.

The power of such responsibility can be observed by those who've been unjustly imprisoned; despite the persecution they faced, they chose to focus inwardly on what brings light, joy, and growth.

This is what my grandpa did, as told in SHACKLED: A Journey From Political Imprisonment To Freedom, when he chose to put his focus towards voraciously studying and gaining wisdom every single day throughout the two decades of darkness, political imprisonment, and family executions he was faced with starting at just six-years-old.

While today, the outside world can look like it has been at its worst in years, we have ever the more reason to attune and polish our inner worlds.

When we are pristinely abundant with life from our inner world, anything we touch in the outer world will be blessed.

THE TRAP OF PROVING YOURSELF

When you let yourself get in the trap of proving yourself, you're stuck with never being yourself.

The only approval you need is within your heart, and it isn't approval so much as it's knowing you're true to yourself and doing the right thing.

It's an unwritten knowing of being true to your nature.

My grandpa says, "You cannot be honest with others until you are first honest with yourself."

There's nothing to prove…to others or yourself.

You need only listen and act from that inner-knowing.

Have faith in the source that made you, that beats within your heart every moment.

HOW TO BE A TRUE ROCKSTAR

The difference between someone who sucks and someone who rocks is this: the person who sucks is sucking the energy from the field, thereby making everyone else feel a drop in energy, where the person who rocks is rocking the baseline energy of the field, propelling people forth to being more awake, aware, excited, energized, and lively.

A true rockstar embodies and integrates the energies of both the grounded presence of earth (rock) and its celestial divinity (star).

May we all be true rockstars, grounded in our humanity and transcendent in our spirituality.

People who suck and people who rock are both agents of change, shaking up the way things are and causing the baseline quality of energy to shift.

Whether we experience constructive growth or a destructive collapse, it all depends on whether energy is being added or subtracted from the field.

Always add more than you take and your life will be growing with abundance.

When the field around us all is rich, we all become rich.

Symptoms of poverty in anything are always in direct relation to the poverty of quality energy in the systems that encompass the field of those affected.

By bringing more quality energy to any system, whether it's your body, family, relationships, community, business, country, or the world, we can upgrade the entire functioning of the system with the most efficiency, effectiveness, and sustainability.

TRUE SUCCESS

While the society we've lived in has valued success by the possessions, status, and material wealth we attain, the truest measure of success is one's own self-actualization.

When you know yourself and live the truth that you are, all that you touch is kissed by the Light within.

When you know truly yourself, you will truly know God.

THE GAME OF THE MIND

We either realize the game of the mind of the mind or become subject to it.

How we realize the game of the mind is by observing its activity.

Notice the thoughts you think like clouds passing in the sky.

Are they even your thoughts?

Where did they come from?

Does it serve you and others to believe them to be real?

How does it serve life to believe them to be real?

The mind is a poor master and an excellent servant.

When the mind is guided by a higher purpose, it becomes obsessively focused on all the details that complement its fulfillment.

Allow your mind to become drunkenly crazed by a vision of Love.

Let it run mad in ecstasy rather than helpless in misery.

Practice witnessing and observing the thoughts that appear in your mind without attaching them to your identity.

Practice this both in silence and activity.

Practice questioning what you believe.

Practice questioning the source, the origin, of where these thoughts are coming from.

Practice being a magnet for greater thoughts.

Practice thinking the thoughts that humanity needs to be thinking.

Practice opening yourself up to thoughts that are evolutionary.

Practice feeling the richness that exists beyond thoughts.

LIBERATING STUCKNESS

When you feel stuck, rather than struggling to get unstuck, put your attention on where you feel stuck.

Feel where in your body there's a sensation of stuckness.

Place your hands over where you feel stuck and allow this stuck area to voice its stuckness.

All stuckness beings with a limited perspective and it affects our physical range of motion, as well as our range of emotion.

By acknowledging and expressing the emotion that feels bound in our body and mind, we liberate what was once stuck into being in harmony with the rest of our body and mind.

Avoiding where and how you feel stuck will only allow the stuckness to persist.

Some ways people seek to avoid this include coping mechanisms and addictions, but another way is by looking for a solution to remove the stuckness.

The quest for an answer, an elixir, something or someone that can save us from our feelings of stuckness is more often than not just another way of avoiding being with the stuckness.

Pain is a messenger with wisdom to share with us, and the stuckness we feel has something valuable to share with us…if only we listen.

Stuckness gives us the gift of realizing we've been living life with a limited perspective.

Only when we're with it, expressing the primal sounds of frustration and being stuck, do we feel the energy move from what once felt bound.

Try this experiment:

If there's an area of your body or life you feel stuck, focus on it and bring your hands over where you feel stuck.

Feel the stuckness and let the emotion express and reverberate through this area.

Take a deep breath and notice what changes in your body and your perspective.

THE ILLUSION OF "TOXIC" MASCULINITY AND FEMININITY

In a society where women are being conditioned to be masculinized and men are being conditioned to feminized, we have a bunch of people living opposite their core nature, experiencing the symptoms and challenges that come with that, and for those who refuse to take part in the craziness…they're often condemned if they live true to their nature.

Masculinity is not toxic, nor is femininity.

They are both energetic aspects of creation that are complements for one another.

Participating in the madness to view one or the other as toxic is what's truly toxic, and it will ensure you repel the complementary energy that your soul craves for in partnership.

Your true nature is what liberates you beyond all programming.

Masculine and feminine are aspects of Creation.

We're designed to attract and be attracted to our opposite complementary energy, but that will never happen if we're not living true to our own nature.

At best, when living opposite one's energetic nature, they'll only attract someone else who's living opposite their own nature as well.

Opposites always want to attract, even if they're twisted from their true face.

In a moment of remembering your nature, all the programming unwinds and you're free again, experiencing the magic of life through you.

This remembering of your essence is nothing you need to learn or read about; it's something innate within you, something you allow to just be.

ANCESTORS

We are the fulfillment to the prayers of our ancestors, and we will be the spark of the fulfilled prayers by our future generations.

We are sacredly interwoven multi-generationally beyond the bounds of time for the purpose of a greater destiny.

Explore your roots and pay attention to the clues in your history.

Create a vision for a legacy you wish to leave for your future generations.

In every moment, we have opportunities to honor, bless, and further impact the world with the gifts of our lineage.

Remember.
Honor.
Expand.
Bless.

AMIDST TIMES OF UNCERTAINTY

In times of uncertainty, the mind will first want answers…a diagnosis…reasons for why things are the way they are.

Then, after the mind seems to have a story for why things are the way they are, it will want solutions on how to fix it.

Often times, the answers that the mind chooses to accept as true are chosen just to give a sense of relief in having some idea or understanding as to what's happening.

This sense of understanding gives the mind the perception of some sense of control.

"At least I know what it is," the mind thinks.

Even if the diagnosis is impending death.

What's more important than accepting any answer given is to ask greater questions and be more curious before jumping to conclusions.

After all, look at all the people diagnosed with terminal cancer who significantly outlived their prognosis because they refused to believe in it.

The mind wants answers.

But we must be wary of this search for answers and the answers that are presented to us.

At best, ideas are placeholders in front of the experience of reality.

Times of uncertainty are calling us to ask more deep, important, and critical questions.

Question the answers you're presented with and question the questions being asked.

Question for the sake of knowing what's true.

STRETCHING

We are taught to stretch our bodies and that with greater flexibility comes greater health, but rarely if ever are we taught to stretch our minds and become more flexible in our mentality.

Limits in the body's range of motion can even be affected with limits in the range of flexibility of the mind, a.k.a. the body mind connection.

If we are incapable of observing our life experiences from more than one perspective, we will bind ourselves to the limits of our mind's focus.

Practice stretching your mind by opening your awareness to more enriching thoughts, ideas, and perspectives.

Stretch your body **and** your mind for greater health.

HAPPINESS

If you can't enjoy and appreciate where you are right now, what makes you think you'll enjoy and appreciate the present moment if/when you're where you want to be?

Maybe you feel like you'll be happy when this happens or that happens, and if that's so, why would you limit how you feel to just happenstance?

Why do you want happiness, which only lasts for moments and is often based on circumstances, when you can have the eternal river of joy move through you and bless all those who are touched by your presence, like the water of life that gives the flowers and trees along its stream more energy to bloom with vitality.

The truth is joy is here and forever now, just waiting for you to remember, reclaim, and share it.

Happiness is temporal and based on if our life matches the blueprint or checklist we have for how things should be.

Most often, this blueprint is not even ours, rather based on our source of love from childhood: the parent or guardian whom we sought love from.

Sometimes it's the polar opposite of both parents.

So the first question is, is your blueprint even your blueprint?

What is it you truly desire?

What will attaining your desires make you feel?

Knowing this, what is it you truly want?

These feelings…emotions…energies?

What are the energies and how can you feel them now, irrespective of circumstances?

Wherever your focus goes, you feel and experience that reality.

At the core, most of us want love, joy, and gratitude, all of which can be experienced here and now.

BREATHING DEEP

Place more attention on the depth of your breath than the thoughts that run through your mind.

The way you breathe affects you biochemically, or in other words, physically, emotionally and mentally.

When you breathe deep with focus, the anxieties of the mind no longer seem like tentacles wrapping around and hijacking your awareness.

You are always in direct control of your focus and must always practice focusing intentionally.

You can bring light to where there's darkness, and you can also expand the light that's already here.

Imagine all the different decisions you could see if at times of stress, instead of reacting, you paused your mind's fretting to breathe deeply.

Breathe deep and full, my friends.

SPIRITUALITY

Some people treat spirituality more like a brand than a practice these days.

They want to look the part, act the part, and yet, there's no "part" to fit into in the first place.

Spirituality is a constant and ever-evolving inquiry into the essence behind the human experience and all creation.

It is an exploration, observation, and relationship with the unseen energies of creation, mastering how with even our pure awareness alone, we can influence great changes in this material dimension.

Spirituality is a journey to knowing thyself, giving the gifts we're called to give, and receiving others as the gifts they are, blessing them by witnessing them in this sacred way.

Here's a simple yet comprehensive take on spirituality:

You don't need yoga, crystals, and meditation to experience the spiritual nature of reality.

You don't need to be a vegan (which isn't even healthy when you look past the marketing buzz), happy all the time, or have any particular political bias to embody your spiritual nature.

You don't need to be anything, do anything, or have anything outside of your own authentic nature to observe, experience, embody and transmit your soul gifts to others.

Spirituality instills both a profound sense of responsibility and surrender in how we live our lives.

Spirituality is not something to achieve, more so a journey of expanding awareness and our contribution to others.

Spirituality is not the utter disregard for the material world, rather the remembrance that all existence came from non-existence, and that the two share a special relationship.

THIS SILENCE

In a moment, this silence cuts through all the noise and reveals what's true.

This silence is not empty.

This silence is all-encompassing, containing all the information that has, does, and will ever exist.

This silence is not difficult to connect with.

This silence is everywhere and within you.

However it is that you connect with this silence, do that more often.

In silence, all beings are One.

In silence, brilliance floods through you, like the sun shining through the window.

In silence, we remember who we are.

QUESTION WHAT YOU SEE AND HEAR

When a population of people are programmed via information to be fearful, anxious, and stressed about the "news", they become more normalized to living with stress-pattern responses that cause them to perceive reality while their sympathetic nervous system is actively engaged.

In this stressed state, their spinal cord is stretched and it becomes more difficult for circulation to flow to the prefrontal cortex to engage the higher cognitive thinking faculties of the brain since the perceived threat, real or not, to the person's survival is what takes precedence over thinking more critically with depth.

Things that would be more obvious in a naturally relaxed state suddenly become less obvious.

Hypocrisies are nullified and correlations are more difficult to make since the only thing that concerns the person in this state is survival.

This is one of the challenges of news programming (and yes,

they even call it news programming): people are reacting to information that's presented to them without taking the time to do their due diligence and determine if it's even true.

In a time where there is more conflicting information than ever before, we must be investigative journalists to find the truth and connect the dots amidst the sea of biased, political-economic agenda-driven noise channeled through a few interconnected corporate conglomerates that own 95% of the media.

If you ever want to know if there's a political-economic agenda to something, use the simple principle of "follow the money".

While there are threats to our survival that we must always pay heedful caution to, we must also be discerning of weaponized information.

The fascinating thing about the truth is it's not biased, nor does it have an agenda.

It's just truth.

We feel it and we know it.

We don't need to be manipulated into a state of fear to believe it.

It is what it is.

Instead of consuming information that is programmed out to us, even if it's from organizations that we like, we must consistently ask ourselves, "What's the truth here?"

ON PROVING OTHERS WRONG

Rather than angrily focusing on the quest to prove others wrong, direct your attention inwards and improve yourself.

Why are you so fervently seeking the approval of others?

This quest to prove another wrong is just another attempt to receive their validation through the desired reaction you want them to have upon witnessing your success; however, this success is primarily only of your exterior shell, not your inner self, especially if you're still living for the opinions of others.

No matter how specially designed you make your ego, no matter what reactions you receive, the same wounded self will be running the show until you tend to your inner world.

Enough with the proving others wrong nonsense.

It's still about proving yourself to them.

The only proving you need to do is improving, and the gratification of that will get you excited to keep growing.

Improving yourself is not limited to improving your outer world.

The true improvements happen when you polish your inner world.

When you change the way you see things, the things you see change.

When you polish the lens through which you see, all that you see is more clear and vivid.

Polish your inner world to the point the inner mirror is so clear, the Light can shine through seamlessly.

TIME IS LIMITED

Your existence will come to an end, this is inevitable.

With every passing moment you are one moment closer to your demise.

The only way you can truly become immortal is if your contributions live beyond your mortality.

We must ask ourselves everyday…what are the most important things I can do today for the legacy I am committed to growing during my life?

The average lifespan is 78.6 years, comprising of 688,536 hours.

If you live to 100 years-old, we're looking at 876,000 hours from the time of birth.

Your time is limited and you must remind yourself of this fact every single day if you want to make the most of it.

Treat your time as sacred by investing it into what brings more value.

LISTEN TO YOUR INNER GUIDANCE COUNSELOR FREQUENTLY

While receiving counsel from others who have more experience is great, the most important counselor we must listen to is our inner guidance counselor.

If you live your life based on the opinions of others, you'll never unravel the magic of life that's uniquely expressed through you.

The unraveling is omnipresently guiding all of us.

You don't need knowledge or skill in how to listen to this guidance.

You only need to listen and act upon it.

Experiences will show you over time that the best decisions you make are the ones that come from your inner-knowing.

THE INTENT OF THE COMMUNICATOR

When you place your attention on how things are being communicated rather than what is being communicated, you uncover why the communicator is communicating their message.

The intent behind the communicator's communicating is what we all need to be focusing on much more often, whether it's a person or an organization.

It is the intent that reveals their outcomes, and the truth is not every person, organization, government, or coalition of governments has intentions that'd be beneficial to you, your family, community, humanity, and the world.

Question why and how things are being said and you'll get to the heart of the matter.

THERE ARE NO FAILURES, ONLY RESULTS

There are no failures.

There are only results.

Some results are greater in quality, others poorer, and most tend to settle for a range their society and culture determine as "normal".

You are responsible for the results you achieve, which means that you are always capable of changing the quality of results by doing greater.

That doing-ness is most sustainable and effortless when you're integrally aligned in your being-ness.

From being true to your nature, your doings are more effective and enjoyable, and greater results will come more effortlessly.

Being-ness guides our doing-ness in the most natural of ways.

THE GIFT OF YOUR MOST PAINFUL EXPERIENCES

If there's at least one gift you can find from the most painful experiences of your life, let it be the gift of empathy and compassion for others who've suffered as well.

Through empathy and compassion, we open a vortex of healing, dignity, and truly seeing one another for both the humanity and spirituality that we are.

Even through the worst we've experienced, we can still make the worst a gift.

By blessing others with a compassionate ear, we absolutely make our worst experiences a gift.

The gift is in what we give.

LIVING TRUTH

It's not that you are speaking truth, it's that you are the living truth.

When you live coherently as the light of truth, all you can see is the truth of what is for what it is.

You recognize others for their nature and can discern when there's incongruence with their true nature.

Like a record scratching, you can spot out the inconsistencies by shining the light of truth.

Like a lighthouse, you become a beacon of soul from the Source that Knows All, that Source that is Omnipresent from the core of your heart.

OVERTHINKING

Overthinking is a defense strategy of the mind to avoid feeling emotions by suppressing your awareness with the clouds of thoughts.

The mind's sense of stability is threatened when emotions outside of your normal range of experience are present, since emotions cause immediate and spontaneous change biochemically, shifting the way we experience and observe reality.

Emotions are not permanent, nor are they something to hide.

When you feel through it, you heal through it, and healing is about becoming more wholesome.

When you notice yourself falling for the trap of overthinking, simply pause, breathe deep, and feel.

We always have the choice to choose higher quality emotions, but we must feel what is present first.

The simple solution to overthinking is this: FEEL.

EMBRACE YOUR PAINS

You complain about the pain in your lower back that's been around since what seems like forever, or the stiffness in your neck and shoulder that's limited your range of motion, but have you ever thought to put your hands over it like a loving friend and listen to what your pains have to tell you?

Have you ever considered that your range of motion could be a physical manifestation of your range of emotion, the range at which you allow energy to freely flow through you without the need to suppress, compress, depress, or oppress it?

All pain is a messenger, not an enemy we need to get rid of.

Listen to the secrets your pain has to tell you, how it wants you to change your life for the better.

Embrace your pains as a guide rather than demons, listening to what they have to share with you, and you may just notice miracles emerge as the solid walls that once felt impenetrable dissipate now that the rivers of life are free to flow through your being once again.

TRAVEL

One of the many gifts of traveling is that when you see a different part of the world, you tend to see a different part of yourself.

As we travel the world, whether it starts with exploring new areas in our town or city, or it extends to neighboring towns or cities, or different states and provinces, or different countries and continents altogether, the newness we see and the familiarity amongst the newness has a special effect on us that reveals both the diversity and oneness of life.

One single experience we have on our travels can change the entire direction of our life.

It can be an idea to start a business inspired by sharing the experience of another culture.

It can be a single person we meet that leads to a life-long relationship.

It can be a site we visit that invokes the artist within us to create a beautiful work.

It can be a new variety of food or drink we try that we bring back with us and pass on to our family and future generations.

It can be the serenity of nature unique to that place that gives us a sacred and timeless experience.

Although the journey seems to be outwards, it always brings us deeper inwards.

The deeper inwards you journey, the more treasure you have to bring outwards.

What is life, after all, but a gift in itself and a gift to share with others.

The greatest gift we can give the world is the gift of being who we truly are, and traveling always helps to deepen our self-realization.

Travel is a gateway to exploring more of both this beautiful world and the beautiful world within.

SYNCHRONICITY

Life organizes everything synchronistically.

Whether we are aware of the synchronicities through all the serendipities that guide our attention is up to us.

We just need to open our eyes and witness what is.

From there, we will see life unfold and bloom magically.

Synchronicities are constantly happening; serendipities help us recognize them.

When we move towards the serendipities, we align with greater rhythms of synchronicity and from that, everything in our lives becomes more enriched, soulful, purposeful, magical, energized, and magnetized.

OBSERVE AND CREATE RATHER THAN REACT AND DESTROY

People laugh at others who take video games so seriously to the point of cursing the game, the players, and even damaging the game system and television or computer monitor.

The observers of the player know that the game is just a game, not the primary reality, and that every game has a set of principles, rules, and mechanics that define its environment and objectives.

That said, who do you think laughs at you when you take this experience we call life so seriously?

Who…what…is watching this avatar you call "you" reacting to the conditions within this reality?

Lighten up.

Focus instead of reacting.

The soul laughs at the ridiculousness of our own doing.

When you observe more, you are in a position to consciously create, rather than unconsciously destroy.

ACKNOWLEDGMENTS

I hope that through writing this book, I have profusely paid acknowledgment and appreciation to the Soul of souls, the Source of life, and to this gift of life that I've been given.

I wish to thank my family for always loving me, for always allowing me from a young age to explore and adventure, and for always being there for me.

And I want to pay an extra tribute to my grandfathers, Khaled Siddiq Khan "Charkhi" (Baba jan) and Nasratullah Khan Malikyar (Dada). These two men played a monumental role in my life. Dada raised me from the time I was a baby, was there to hear my first words, and was with me almost everyday until I left for University. Dada was a very cheerful soul. He did everything to be there for his family and his grandchildren, regularly referring to us at the joy of his life. He was there with me for countless soccer, baseball, and basketball games, as well as my Karate tournaments, musical performances, you name it. If I was there, he was there. The amount of treasured memories and lessons I've had with Dada are immeasurable.

As for Baba jan, we share such a deep spiritual bond. Like Rumi and Shams, we spent so many years talking about the mystery of life, God, philosophy, and mysticism. I will always treasure the days we'd listen to Nainawaz's music for hours, talking about the deeper meanings and joy of life. Baba jan named me Adam because he said in his lifetime, he didn't see too many actualized humans and decided we have to start over again. Thus, he named me Adam, after the biblical first man.

So long as I'm alive, writing, and have books in print, you both will always be remembered. I'm looking forward to finishing my memoir so I can share with the world the treasured memories we got to have together. Until we meet again, Dada and Baba jan.

ABOUT THE AUTHOR

Adam Malik Siddiq is a passionate soul who can't help himself but keep writing about the grand mystery, adventure, and wisdom of life.

Adam is a multi-award-winning author and narrator with plans to continue writing more works of art that inspires people all around the world to live fully.

He is the host of the Rumi Poems podcast on Spotify with over 100 published episodes and videos reciting Rumi's poetry.

For more of Adam's writings and recordings, be sure to follow him on Instagram, YouTube, and Facebook @theadamsiddiq.

ALSO BY ADAM MALIK SIDDIQ

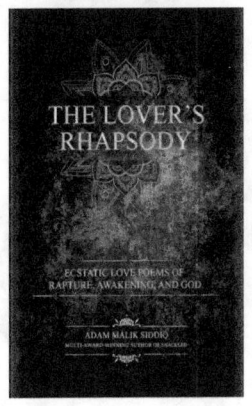

www.ingramcontent.com/pod-product-compliance
Lightning Source LLC
Chambersburg PA
CBHW072004110526
44592CB00012B/1202